IMAGES
of America

TEATOWN
LAKE RESERVATION

Lincoln Diamant

ARCADIA

First printed in 2002.

Published by Arcadia Publishing,
an imprint of Tempus Publishing, Inc.
2A Cumberland Street
Charleston, SC 29401

Printed in Great Britain.

Library of Congress Catalog Card Number: 2002106583

For all general information contact Arcadia Publishing at:
Telephone 843-853-2070
Fax 843-853-0044
E-Mail sales@arcadiapublishing.com

For customer service and orders:
Toll-Free 1-888-313-2665

Visit us on the internet at http://www.arcadiapublishing.com

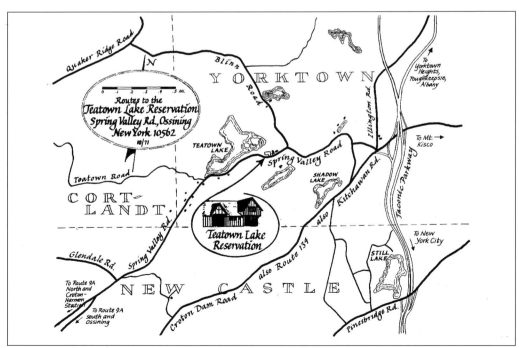

Teatown Lake Reservation, a 759-acre nature preserve, is located in the towns of Cortlandt, New Castle, and Yorktown.

CONTENTS

ACKNOWLEDGMENTS

For the past 40 years, thousands of volunteers have labored mightily with heart and hand to establish and maintain Teatown Lake Reservation as an invaluable community resource, open to all. To salute them by name, with their nourishing contributions, would leave room for little else in this book, itself a labor of love. "The spirit of Teatown," as Jerry Swope used to call it, is what this country is all about—a happy intersection of private and public satisfactions. Without the understanding, cooperation, and hard work of the members of the Teatown History Committee, the author—whose name preempts the title page—would have found the work impossible. Collective thanks are due to Eileen Argenziano, Midge Arnold, Chuck Davidson, Ellen Elchlepp, Susan Jeffers, Sophie Keyes, Sandy Koppen, West Moss, Geoffrey Thompson, Ellan Young, and the tireless committee chair, Jean Cameron-Smith. Appreciation is also due to current and former staff members: Warren Balgooyen, Phyllis Bock, Rod Christie, Edward Kanze, Ruth Rubenstein, and Kenneth Soltesz. This book also requires a special thank-you to all the unidentifiable and identified photographers who contributed so handsomely to its preparation. Finally, a special tip of the hat (for her 11th anniversary at Teatown) goes to the reservation's most able and amiable executive director, Gail Abrams.

Youngsters go for a hayride during Teatown's 1978 Fall Festival. (Photograph by Gerard Swope Jr.)

INTRODUCTION

At a time when modern technology and fast-paced growth have altered the character of many communities with housing developments, shopping centers, and cellular telephone towers, Teatown Lake Reservation has created and fostered a community often referred to as Westchester's "Central Park." Through its nature center exhibits, teacher workshops, school and outreach programs, seminars, birthday parties, special events, and land protection efforts, Teatown fulfills its mission "to conserve open space and to educate and involve the regional community in order to sustain the diversity of wildlife, plants, and habitats for future generations."

Not only has Teatown educated children of all ages, families, youth groups, and adults, but it has also trained many of today's leaders in the field of environmental education and land conservation. Many people who spent a part of their life as Teatown staff members are now writers, educators, executive directors, and leaders in other parts of Westchester County and beyond. As they have learned from Teatown, Teatown has benefited from their dedication, support, and commitment.

Teatown's growth into a regional environmental resource is a result of the work of its professional staff, as well as the hard work and energy through the years of thousands of volunteers. These volunteers have served on the Teatown Board of Trustees, taught schoolchildren, given tours of Wildflower Island, assisted the clerical staff, built bridges, and maintained Teatown's buildings and trails. Without this dedicated cadre of volunteers, Teatown would not be the organization it is today.

We invite you to experience one of Westchester's hidden treasures. Come for a hike, an education program, a seasonal event, or to visit our birds of prey and other live animals on exhibit at our nature center. You will find it difficult to imagine that you are only 40 miles outside of New York City.

—Gail Abrams
Executive Director, Teatown Lake Reservation

Gail Abrams poses with her feathered friend Frosty the screech owl. (Photograph by Ellan Young.)

FACTS, FIGURES, FOLKLORE

Teatown, a nature preserve and education center, has as its mission to conserve open space and to educate and involve the regional community in order to sustain the diversity of wildlife, plants, and habitats for future generations.

Teatown Lake Reservation
1600 Spring Valley Road
Ossining, NY 10562
(Westchester County, Town of Yorktown)
Phone: (914) 762-2912
Fax: (914) 762-2890
Web site: www.teatown.org
E-mail: teatown@teatown.org

- Originally established in 1963, by a 194-acre gift from the Swope family, as an outreach station of the Brooklyn Botanic Garden, New York City. Achieved independent status on July 4, 1987.
- Now a private not-for-profit membership organization administered by an elected board of trustees.
- Individual and family dues-paying membership in 2002: 1,800.
- Grounds open dawn to dusk daily; offices, gift shop closed on Monday.
- Admission is free. Contributions are tax deductible.
- Acreage in 2002: 759, including the Cliffdale Farm section (160 acres) and the Glendale Swamp section (38 acres).
- Teatown Lake (33 acres). No fishing, swimming, or boating.
- All plants and wildlife are 100 percent protected.
- Wildflower Island (2 acres), tours given by trained guides at scheduled times.
- Auditorium, meeting rooms.
- Annual events (adults and children): environmental and nature study programs, lectures, and symposia; history videos available; summer camp; field trips and tours; spring plant sale; Fall Festival; Night in the Woods auction gala; concerts.
- Hiking trails (no bikes): 14.5 miles. No camping. Pets tight-leashed.
- Highest point: Overlook Trail (620 feet). Lowest point: Bailey Brook and Blinn Road (280 feet).

Whence Teatown? There appears to be no geographical antecedent for the name Teatown anywhere in Great Britain or British North America. The Revolutionary tradition persists that a Manhattan greengrocer named John Arthur moved all his stock to this area of Westchester to escape the British troops occupying New York City. Word soon leaked out locally that the grocer had carried with him several chests of priceless tea that he hoped to sell at an enormous profit. The neighborhood women quickly laid siege to Arthur's farmhouse, while he slipped out the back door. Later, he arranged a compromise and agreed to sell them the tea they loved so much at a fair price. Thus arose the name Teatown. (Illustration by Susan Jeffers.)

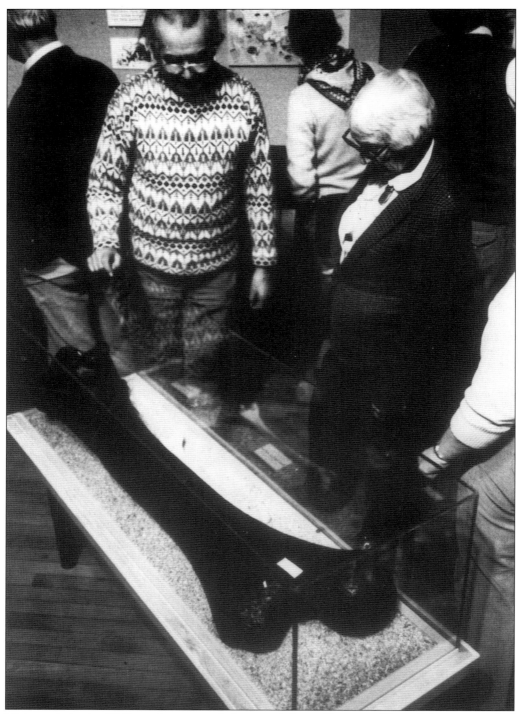

Visitors study the 1986 wooly mammoth bones exhibit at Teatown. The exhibit consisted of bones that were found locally during excavation of the intersection of Route 134 and the Taconic Parkway.

One
ROCKS, RILLS, AND ICE

The New York region is one of the most geologically exciting places in the world. It is well worth the time for anyone with an interest in natural history to learn the basics. Although the language of geology is one of the most esoteric known to the world of science, most of the principles are very straightforward and easy to understand.

The formation of the Appalachian Mountain belt and the effects of the most recent Ice Age contributed most to the topography we see today. More than 500 million years ago, at the end of the Precambrian epoch, the continents split apart and the ancestral Atlantic Ocean was born. When the Atlantic stopped opening and began to close, the compression caused the deep-sea deposits to become altered under heat and pressure. These altered sediments were thrust up to form the ancient Appalachians.

Appreciating all these geological events and the time it took to create today's landscape should inspire us to look more closely at the metamorphic rocks of Westchester. Walking down the paths and trails of Teatown Lake Reservation, we are constantly reminded, by rocky ridges and large blocks of stone, of the glacial action on the reservation's landscape. At many places, the rocky debris suggests a giant's stone blocks, plucked loose by the glacier and flung about in random fashion, ready to be thrown back into some enormous stone toy box. Yet, all of this helter-skelter, rocky pattern is only 12,000 years old—glacially speaking, a wink of the eye.

For thousands of years, a slow-moving, grinding, continental glacier continued to strip southern New England (and Teatown) of its bountiful topsoil. It eventually dumped this load, like passengers streaming off an escalator, into the coastal waters of the Atlantic Ocean. When the rate of glacial melt-back matched the rate of advance for a substantial length of time, offshore islands were formed, including Long Island, Martha's Vineyard, and Nantucket. As the ice sheet slowly retreated northward (past Teatown), it trailed a thin veneer of topsoil amid rocky outcrops—a paltry recompense for all that had been stripped away.

Some scientists believe we are living in the midst of another glacial advance; others argue we are still at the tail end of the last Ice Age. As our climate warms, partially due to the greenhouse effect, we may witness the rising of oceans and the flooding of our harbors. One thing is certain, only time will tell.

Geologic Time Line			
PRECAMBRIAN 4,600*	PALEOZOIC 500-430* 430-395*	MESOZOIC 225-190*	CENOZOIC 2-.01*
Earth's crust, gneiss formed Oceans developed	Ocean sediment turns into marble and schist Rifting and expansion of continents	Land basins and sandstone formed	Glaciation, much erosion; Formation of Long Island, Croton Point, Martha's Vineyard
*Millions of years ago	~~~~~Represents major gaps in time		

This geologic timeline condenses the earth's history.

Gneiss, a metamorphic rock, has been used as a building stone in the nature center. This rock is thought to be more than a billion years old. (Photograph by Ellan Young.)

Pegmatite formations, areas with large quartz and feldspar crystals, are hard to miss in the Teatown area and are most apparent in the rock formations around Teatown Lake. They are approximately 450 million years old. (Photograph by Ellan Young.)

Two
ROCK THROUGH THE AGES

Essay by Ruth Rubenstein

Have you ever taken the time to know a rock, to touch it and feel its texture? We often marvel at high peaks and large rock formations or take notice of the imposing mansions, beautiful churches, and stone walls in our neighborhoods. Yet the rocks around us, the ones in our backyard, remain inconspicuous and undemanding, which is why we probably pass them by without noticing.

More than a billion years of mountain building, erosion, and continental shifting have helped shape the tiny part of the landscape that is now Teatown Lake Reservation. Westchester County consists of three different kinds of rocks: Fordham gneiss (pronounced "nice"), Inwood marble, and Manhattan mica schist. All three of these rocks are metamorphic (have been transformed by heat and pressure) and speak to the amazing geological activity of the past. It is humbling to think that when we scramble around the rocks of Teatown, we are walking on the "stumps" of great mountain ranges that once existed in this area.

The Fordham gneiss found at Teatown is part of the ancient continental crust and is thought to be more than a billion years old. This rock was formed when the proto–North America continent, located near the equator, moved northward as a floating continental plate. When this plate, essentially the Canadian Shield, collided with the next plate, the collision raised mountains and deformed rocks. The offshore sandy sediments that existed as these plates collided were contorted and transformed into gneiss. If we went back in time, we would witness a far different world. There were no blue skies. There were lightning strikes and substantial volcanic activity. The air smelled of sulfur, and the sky was yellowish. This was the age of primitive life known as the Precambrian. It was a time when the atmosphere was changing to include oxygen.

Some 600 million years ago, the basic gneiss was covered by the ocean. Thick layers of limestone sediment from seashells and other marine animals and eroded shale were deposited on top of the gneiss. This area was underwater, and life consisted of primitive fish and trilobites.

About 450 million years ago, new landmasses collided as an offshore volcanic chain thrust into the edge of North America. The high temperatures and pressures hardened the sedimentary layers and metamorphosed them into Inwood marble (transformed limestone) and Manhattan mica schist (transformed shale). This collision formed the Taconic Mountains, which were once an impressive mountain range.

During this period of mountain building, lavalike magma flowed in between the fissures and cracks of the metamorphic rocks or even melted its own path through the stone, allowing pegmatites to form. Pegmatite is essentially the same as granite, except that it has intruded between existing rock layers and taken a much longer time to cool, causing the crystals to become extremely large. The pegmatite formations, areas with large quartz and feldspar crystals, are most apparent in the rock formations around Teatown Lake.

Some 360 million years ago, further continental collisions uplifted and crumpled the plate edges. During this mountain-building event, a supercontinent called Pangea was formed. Great forests consisting of numerous scale trees and seed ferns were everywhere. These forests later decayed and were buried under sediments that succumbed to great pressure transforming them into coal. Giant dragonflies with wingspans of three feet and huge millipedes roamed this part of the earth.

Around 250 million years ago, this crumpling created North American mountains as high as the Rockies. Then, 50 million years after the mountains were created, the plates separated once again, causing huge cracks, or rift valleys, that extend north and south along the coastline. The Hudson River did not carve the Hudson River Valley. Neither did the glaciers. Instead, it was a structural valley that was later occupied by the Hudson River and then by glaciers. The area resembled Death Valley or the African Rift Valley. Vegetation was minimal and consisted of drought-tolerant species. During the age of dinosaurs, the landscape consisted of sand dunes.

This area, which includes Teatown, has since undergone extensive erosion that continues today. Wind, rain, snow, and ice have worn down the mountains. At least four separate ice sheets have passed over the area in the last two million years like huge sandpaper blocks smoothing out the landscape, like a bulldozer pushing sediments ahead of it, and like a sled carrying boulders and rocks and dumping them. The last of these, the Wisconsin glaciation, occurred 12,000 years ago. An ice sheet taller than the Empire State Building scraped out grooves and scratched and polished the surface of outcrops.

The next time you go for a walk, think about the rocks you often take for granted beneath your feet. Just imagine all they have seen: yellow skies, deserts, dinosaurs, tundra, giant mammoths, Revolutionary soldiers, and us. Rocks go further back than our own folklore, stories, and history. Only the rocks really know.

Schist, a metamorphic rock, is commonly used in stone walls throughout the area. (Photograph by Ellan Young.)

Todd Baldwin, former Teatown naturalist, demonstrates the old-fashioned way of cutting ice on Teatown Lake. (Photograph by Ellan Young.)

Winter at Teatown brings fun on the ice.

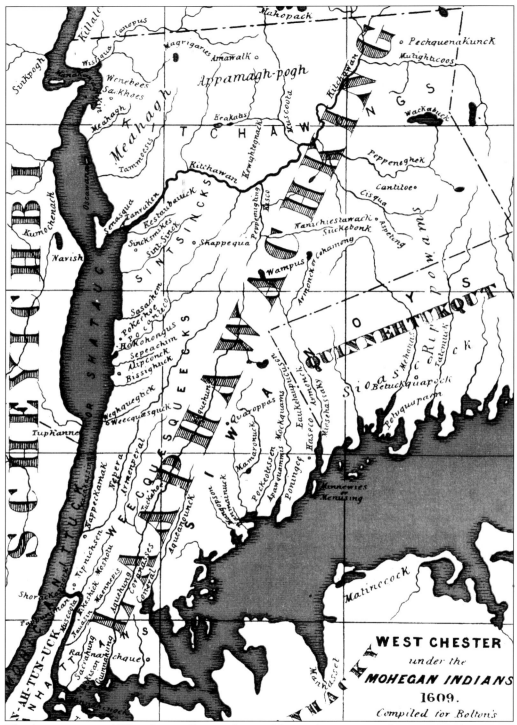

This historic map of Westchester County depicts Native American settlements. Modern name usage may vary.

Three
NATIVE GROUNDS

Following on the heels of the retreating ice came the slow regrowth of grasses, plants, shrubs, and eventually hardwoods and conifers. Once again, the countryside became fit for human habitation, and Native American tribes moved northward after the retreating ice, some ending up even north of the St. Lawrence River.

The Native Americans who lived in clusters throughout the river valley were part of the Algonquin language family. They called themselves the Muhheakunnuk, based on their name for what would eventually be known as the Hudson River, the "river that flows both ways," which is tidal for 150 miles upstream. Europeans later transliterated that name into Mahican, not to be confused with Mohegan, a native group in southern New England.

In the forests, game was plentiful, including deer, bear, moose, beaver, bobcat, otter, mink, rabbit, raccoon, and turkey. At Croton Point on the Hudson River were oysters, mussels, and many varieties of fish. The Kitchawank nation, who lived along the banks of the Croton River and in a palisaded settlement on Croton Point, actively hunted the game found in the forest that now includes Teatown Lake Reservation.

In social organization and tribal relationships, the Mahican way of life was not unlike that of the Mohawks, the nations to the west with whom they were constantly at war. The Mahican settlements consisted of a group of bark shelters, or longhouses, similar to today's exhibit at Cliffdale Farm, each usually containing three families with three fireplaces. Each village included about 200 natives. In today's terms, the entire region was sparsely populated; the total Mahican population was around 4,500. Every decade or so, the location of villages was moved, due to the impoverishment of soils near the settlement, plus shortages of firewood and an increasing quantity of waste and general refuse. Around the villages, the natives girdled the trees, burned the deadwood, and planted their modest gardens between the charred stumps. During the growing season, garden yield was substantial, including maize, squash, and beans (the "Three Sisters") and probably sunflowers. In the event of a poor growing season or a scarcity of game, the winter could be a time of great privation. Horticulture was primarily the work of women. In the springtime, schools of spawning Atlantic herring, shad, and striped bass ran up the Hudson and its tributaries, keeping the men busy fishing with nets and weirs along the shore while the women seeded the gardens. During the summer and fall, the women gathered berries and nuts in the woods for careful storage in grass- or bark-lined pits. In the early spring, flocks of migrating passenger pigeons (now extinct) provided an abundant food supply.

Sachems and under sachems were empowered to govern the tribe or nation, determining land use, resolving arguments, enforcing their decisions, presiding over rites and ceremonies, and organizing the group's protection. Kinship among the Kitchawanks was traced through the female line. In the case of family separation, the children remained with the mother. The distribution of produce from a cultivated garden was matrilinear; what the women sowed, cultivated, and harvested was distributed by them to the rest of the group. Early Europeans mistakenly regarded this control as a form of private property, the basis of white society, and that caused much mutual misunderstanding.

Thus, for several millennia the Kitchawanks spent their lives in a landscape whose broader outlines were not much different from ours today, except that the waters were cleaner, the forests were deeper, and the geese and deer were fewer.

A Native American carries a basket of maize, squash, and beans—the "Three Sisters." (Illustration by Susan Jeffers.)

The longhouse (above) and the wigwam (below) constructed at Cliffdale Farm are used for exhibition and education programs.

A fanciful portrait of Henry Hudson shows the arrival of the *Half-Moon* in the Hudson River. (From the archives of the Croton Historical Society.)

An old print depicts Henry Hudson meeting the local native sachem and fellow Kitchawank tribesmen at Croton Point, which was also known as Teller's Point in earlier days.

Four
HERE COME THE DUTCH

"If you see strangers come by the side of your fireplace, you must be friendly to them, for you, too, will be a stranger some time or other."—Muhheakunnuk teaching.

By the middle of the 16th century, huge and clumsy white-winged European vessels were not unknown to Native Americans along the northeastern Atlantic coast. Spanish carracks and caravels, pinnaces and grand galleons—homebound from looting Mexico, Central America, and South America (by way of the Panamanian isthmus)—would occasionally sail by the offshore sandbars, blown northward from their trade wind course.

However, the mouth of the great Mahicanituck River seemed to hold little interest for any of these strange ships. Only once, in the early 1500s, an Italian who was sailing for a French king briefly threaded the shoals that guarded its spacious harbor. Giovanni da Verrazano never returned to the great river he discovered in 1524, but the legend of his peaceful visit was mingled with 10 centuries of tribal lore of the Muhheakunnuk people.

Some 85 years later, another vessel tacked north against a contrary breeze into the broad estuary. It was the tiny *Halve-Maen* (*Half-Moon*), captained by the English explorer Henry Hudson, on a haphazard voyage of exploration to find a shortened route to the cloves and spices of the Moluccas.

The story of the crucial first encounters between the *Half-Moon*'s disorderly crew and the Muhheakunnuk "River Indians" must rely on two eyewitness accounts, both published independently—in England and Holland—16 years after Hudson's voyage. Any other record that ever existed has disappeared into the dustbin of history. By 1841, when New York State officially sought to recover from Holland additional Dutch East and West India Company documents dealing with the discovery and settlement of New Netherland, the Dutch government had just auctioned and scattered all the pertinent papers. One can assume the priceless relics were used either to wrap herring or to light fires. Nothing new on Hudson's explorations—or, indeed, on Hudson himself—has surfaced since.

In 1625, Hudson's own now vanished journal still lay open in Leiden, in front of the eminent geographer (and director of the newly formed Dutch West India Company) Johannes de Laet, as he labored over *Nieuw Wereld,* his monumental real estate promotion of all the knowledge of North America brought back by early European explorers. Part of de Laet's 10th chapter actually quotes Henry Hudson—the only direct words we shall ever have from this superb navigator, who captained tiny, scummy crews to the farthest reaches of the North Atlantic, accommodating mutiny after mutiny until the final uprising that put a theatrical end to his life.

Hudson arrived inside Sandy Hook on September 4, 1609. During 20 of the next 28 days, he and his crew were in contact with the Muhheakunnuk people along the river—days marked by fear, kidnapping, and bloodshed, only occasionally interspersed with visions of the peaceful coexistence de Laet was later able to extract from Hudson's journal, "sufficient reason for me to conclude that with mild and proper treatment, and especially by intercourse with Christians, this people might be civilized and brought under better regulation."

The *Half-Moon* was blown—or laboriously tacked—up a crooked stretch of what soon proved (with a jolt) to be no passage at all, but a unique and deceptive 150-mile-long fjord, which Hudson mistook for the ice-free intercontinental strait.

On September 24, 1609, a party went ashore, and de Laet quotes Hudson, "the natives are a very good people, for when they saw that I would not remain, they supposed I was afraid of their bows. Taking the arrows, they broke them into pieces and threw them into the fire." Hudson had nothing but praise for the new land he had discovered. "Their land is the finest for cultivation that I ever in my life set foot upon."

Hudson's important discovery for the Dutch was resented by the English, who placed him under genteel house arrest. However, the Amsterdam merchants proved far more interested in the market potential of native furs than in any of the explorer's recorded suggestions for permanent settlement.

Barred from trading with the "foreigners" in Canada and Virginia, the Dutch entrepreneurs and their captains were content to simply sail in and out of their great river for almost a dozen years, exchanging goods for furs at arm's length with the Muhheakunnuk and their hereditary enemies, the Mohawk Nations. Then, undoubtedly spurred by news of the English establishment of a colony on a large rock in eastern Massachusetts, the Estates General approved the formation of the Dutch West India Company, with full economic and political responsibility for New Netherlands. However, it was not until May 1624 that the first Dutch colonizing ship arrived in Lower Bay, carrying 30 families, mostly Walloons, to plant a true Dutch colony along both banks of the river Hudson had discovered. From then on, the settlement and expansion of New Netherlands was slow but steady. Among the earliest immigrants (1638) to the new colony was Oloff Stevenszen and his wife, Anneken, whose son, Stephanus, was born in 1643. Stevenszen later changed the family surname to Van Cortlandt to honor the Dutch place of his birth.

Stephanus Van Cortlandt (1643–1700) became an important merchant and politician who held high posts, including mayor of New York City. At a time when the Dutch Estates General (united states) commanded one of Europe's great navies, it was easy for Holland to keep New Netherlands under her skirts for more than half a century. By the 1660s, however, as Dutch sea power declined, New Amsterdam became too tempting a prize for the British to ignore. In 1664, reflecting a wider European war, a British squadron sailed into the harbor and captured the colony from Gov. Pieter Stuyvesant without a shot being fired.

Van Cortlandt was a councilor for many years, judge of the admiralty court, and associate justice of the provincial supreme court, of which he was appointed chief justice shortly before his death. In 1697, he was granted a royal patent from King William III, making his upriver estates the equivalent of an English manor. With the grant came the responsibility of providing his tenant farmers with a schoolteacher, minister, and miller. Van Cortlandt himself served as judge and jury in both civil and criminal cases.

The greater part of Van Cortlandt's estate was an 86,000-acre tract extending for 10 miles along the east bank of the Hudson River from Croton Point to Anthony's Nose and as far back into the eastern woods as the Connecticut boundary. What today is Teatown was included in this original patent.

Shortly after receiving his grant, Van Cortlandt died. For many years his widow, Gertrude, busied herself with managing the vast estate from her home in New York City. The manor's population was spread thin. Fewer than 100 tenant families lived on Van Cortlandt Manor; one of the tenants farmed a large hilly area that now includes Teatown Lake Reservation.

Philip Van Cortlandt, born in 1683 the son of Stephanus and Gertrude, married Catharine, the daughter of Abraham De Peyster. Upon the widow Van Cortlandt's death in 1723, surveyors were commissioned to divide Van Cortlandt Manor into equal shares for the 10 surviving children.

In 1749, Pierre Van Cortlandt (1721–1814), the fourth generation of this dynasty of Manhattan merchants, moved with his wife, Joanna, and young son, Philip, from New York City to his inherited section of the estate, a 1,225-acre tract with a home (the Van Cortlandt Manor house) on the Croton River. Pierre Van Cortlandt became Croton's first commuter, sailing his ships regularly back and forth to New York City.

When the Declaration of Independence separated the colonies from Great Britain in 1776, all of Van Cortlandt Manor—together with Teatown—became part of the new United States of America. Pierre Van Cortlandt truly believed in the new nation. He served it well and soon became New York's first lieutenant governor, under George Clinton. He lived on in Croton until 1814. Where they could, the Van Cortlandt tenants bought outright the land that they, their parents, and grandparents had been farming for many years.

A coat of arms was a necessity for anyone owning a manor. Stephanus Van Cortlandt developed this one. (*Van Cortlandt Coat of Arms,* oil and gold leaf on a wooden panel, by G. Kane, probably of New York, *c.* 1790–1825; courtesy Historic Hudson Valley, Tarrytown, New York.)

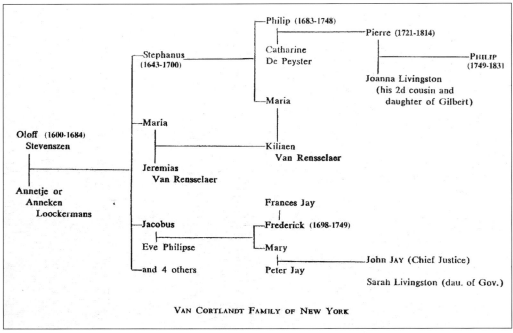

Philip (1683-1748)

Catharine
De Peyster

Pierre (1721-1814)

PHILIP
(1749-1831

Joanna Livingston
(his 2d cousin and
daughter of Gilbert)

Stephanus
(1643-1700)

Maria

Oloff (1600-1684)
Stevenszen

Maria

Kiliaen
Van Rensselaer

Jeremias
Van Rensselaer

Annetje or
Anneken
Loockermans

Frances Jay

Jacobus

Frederick (1698-1749)

Eve Philipse

Mary

and 4 others

John JAY (Chief Justice)

Peter Jay

Sarah Livingston (dau. of Gov.)

VAN CORTLANDT FAMILY OF NEW YORK

A family tree shows the lineage of the Van Cortlandts of New York.

This portrait of Pierre Van Cortlandt was done in oils on canvas by an unknown artist *c.* 1730. It is 57$^{1}/_{2}$ by 41$^{5}/_{8}$ inches. (Brooklyn Museum of Art, Dick S. Ramsay Fund.)

The 18th-century Van Cortlandt Manor house was the primary residence of the Van Cortlandt family. It was not only the country seat but also a working estate that was economically successful.

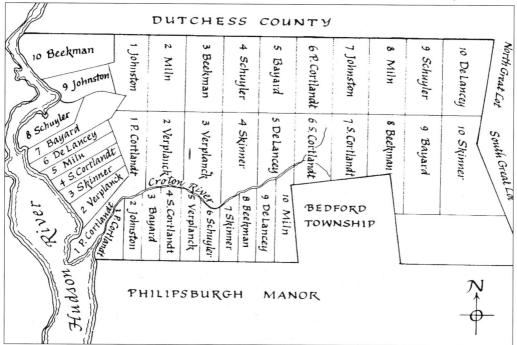

This map shows the partition of Van Cortlandt Manor among the heirs of Stephanus Van Cortlandt (Cortlandt's first subdivision). Teatown is located in Great Lot 3, south of the Croton River.

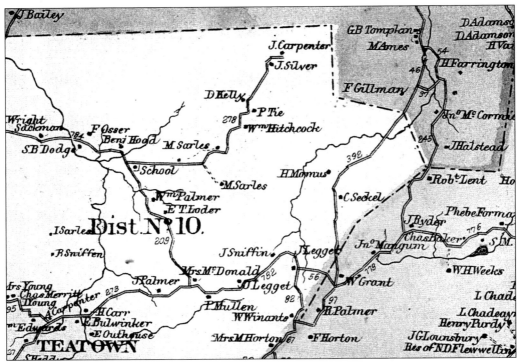

This 1872 map of Yorktown shows the Teatown vicinity.

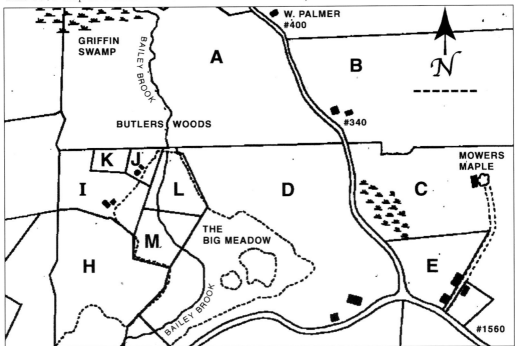

This plot map of the Teatown area indicates the various holdings described in the following chapter, from the 1700s to 1963.

Five

FARMERS IN THE DELL

Shouldering up against the north and south limits of Stephanus Van Cortlandt's 10-mile-long by 20-mile-deep royal grant were the far greater holdings of the Philipse family, with a pie slice of New Castle thrown in. At that time, the Philipse (formerly Dutch Flypse) fortune was the largest in British North America, and Frederick Philipse III was an unshakable Royalist. It should come as no surprise that the entire Philipse clan was both prosecuted and persecuted by patriots during the American Revolution. For a time, near blind Frederick Philipse III was imprisoned in the Simsbury lead mine in Connecticut; all the Philipses eventually fled to England. Unlike the landholdings of the patriotic Van Cortlandts, which remained untouched, every piece of Philipse property was forfeited to the new state of New York to be immediately auctioned among the tenant farmers who actually worked the soil. Thus was New York State's treasury born.

Things were quite different on Van Cortlandt Manor as Pierre Van Cortlandt began to sell off parts of his inherited lands, which included the present location of Teatown Lake Reservation. The complicated two-century record of land sales and transfers outlined in this chapter may seem daunting, but it is important to realize that our entire society is built on the execution and preservation of such meticulous land ownership records. We hope the material that follows, therefore, will be of interest not just to genealogists.

The earliest known purchaser of the Teatown property (c. 1780) was William Palmer, who converted a dairy barn into a farmhouse on what became Blinn Road, named in the 20th century after actor Holbrook Blinn. Farther down Blinn Road was Bailey Brook, named after James Bailey, who built a wire mill at the confluence of the brook and the Croton River. The Bailey property was wiped out by the Croton Dam flood in 1841. The brook flowed out of Griffin Swamp, named after one-armed James Griffin, who in 1851 bought a three-acre plot of land on the north side of Apple Bee Farm Road, where he built his home. He later acquired another 75 acres south of the road. This property, which extended southward to the swamp, was finally sold by Delia Griffin, who was either his wife or his daughter-in-law.

In 1826, William Palmer deeded 91 acres (plots A and B on the map) to his son Robert. Some 29 years later, Robert Palmer sold these plots to Jacob Willets. Three years after that, Willets sold his holdings to Elias Loder, who lived on the property for 22 years, selling plot A in 1880. The property then had a succession of several short-term owners until 1891, when it was purchased by Elmer T. Butler, who owned it throughout the early 1900s but apparently never lived there; his home was on Staten Island. Jesse Wynants of Ossining, who lived in this area as a child, said the property below the 1924 Teatown Lake dam was then known as Butler's Woods.

Robert Palmer's plot B had a different history. The farmhouse, at 340 Blinn Road, was built in the 1820s by Robert Palmer. In 1855, the land was purchased by Jacob Willets and, in 1858, it was sold to Elias Loder. Loder lived in the house and farmed the land until it was sold c. 1900 to Labolt Rickard, who farmed it until he died in the 1920s. It was bought by Gerard Swope Sr. in 1928 from Rickard's son, Leslie. Blueberry Pond, adjoining the house, was built by Gerard Swope Jr. in 1950.

In 1832, William Palmer deeded plot C to Robert Palmer's older brother, John. John Palmer already owned the land across Blinn Road to the west—plots D, L, and M. The only building on plot C at that time was an old barn. According to an aerial photograph taken c. 1930, the red maple swamp on the west side of plot C was recently an open marsh.

The 50-acre plot D represents the main portion of the John Palmer farm. Early deeds to this land are not available, but Palmer probably acquired the plot from his father in 1832. He lived with his wife, Deborah, in a house that according to early maps was situated about where Teatown's renovated administration building is today. Palmer's barn stood where Teatown's maple sugaring shed now stands. It was removed c. 1915. The imbedded twist-wire fences that still remain attached to some larger trees seem to be characteristic of this farm. Part of the property now flooded by the construction of Teatown Lake in 1924 is referred to in some old deeds as the Big Meadow.

John Palmer bequeathed his farm to his son, Ezra J. Palmer, in 1872. Ezra Palmer mortgaged the land, unhappily defaulted on the mortgage, and the courts auctioned the farm in 1889. At this time, the farm included plots C, D, and F, a total of 120 acres. The high bid of $2,500 was submitted by Martin Niland. The property then went through a series of owners: Martin Niland to Mary Moses (date unknown); Mary Moses to Fanny Herschfield, 1893; Herschfield estate to Arthur S. Vernay, 1915; Marion K. Vernay to Dan Hanna, 1919.

The Tudor structures that are now Teatown's administrative center were built c. 1920 by Dan Hanna, nephew of Ohio politician Mark Hanna. Dan Hanna died in 1922.

Plot E, originally two acres, was purchased from John Palmer by Michael Seitz in 1868. Another three acres were purchased in 1875. Michael Seitz was a dairy farmer; the property was not large enough for other types of farming. When Seitz died, the farm was left to his children, Ralph and Mollie Seitz. In 1932, the farm passed to Charles Cummings, the husband of Alma Seitz, Ralph's daughter. In 1935, the land was deeded to Henrietta Hill and, in 1937, Hill sold it to his neighbor Gerard Swope Sr.

Plot F was part of the John Palmer farm that had been auctioned by the courts to Martin Niland in 1889. Niland apparently did not live there but retained ownership until 1912, when he sold to Walter S. Stern. That same year, Stern sold to Arthur S. Vernay and his wife, Marion. Vernay was an antiques dealer from New York City. He was also a big-game hunter and spent 10 years in Africa collecting specimens for the American Museum of Natural History (his name is still displayed on a plaque in the museum's Roosevelt Wing). He built the Croft in 1913, furnishing the interior with English antiques. The fireplace mantel, for instance, is carved oak dated 1357.

Upon Vernay's death, Marion Vernay sold the property to Dan Hanna in 1919, and Mollie Hanna sold it to Gerard Swope Sr. in 1922. After his father died in 1957, Gerard Swope Jr., as executor of the estate, sold the Croft residence to Phil Gilbert.

Plot G, approximately 30 acres, was purchased by John Kahrs in 1860. Herman Kahrs, John's brother, who inherited the holding, sold the farm sometime in the early 1900s. The Herman Kahr house was located on the north side of Spring Valley Road near the Bailey Brook inlet to Teatown Lake.

Plot H, now flooded by Teatown Lake, was owned by Ezra J. Palmer, who sold it in 1848 to John Vail. Vail sold it to Stansbury Lawrence around 1870, and it eventually became part of the Walter T. Stern holdings, which were purchased by Arthur S. Vernay in 1912 and later passed to Dan Hanna. Gerard Swope Sr. acquired it in 1922.

Plots I, J, and K, approximately 12 acres, were sold by Richard Palmer, another son of William Palmer, to Burnett Palmer for the sum of $264.50. Some 11 years later, Burnett Palmer sold the plots to Baker Sniffen, who lived there with his wife, Mary, from 1837 until he died in 1874. His son, Allen Sniffen, built another house, located a short distance to the north and east. In 1844, Baker Sniffen deeded the property surrounding his house, the one-acre plot J, to Allen Sniffen. In 1853, Allen Sniffen and his wife, Elizabeth, sold the acre to Isaac Sarles. In 1890, Isaac and Eliza Sarles's son, Orson, and his wife, Margaret Ann, sold the entire 12 acres, plots I, J, and K, to Ann and James Outhouse. In 1909, the Outhouses sold this parcel to John Malone, who lived on Spring Valley Road near the west end of Teatown Lake. All of Malone's landholdings were sold to Gerard Swope Sr. in 1924.

Plots L and M, four acres each, were adjuncts to the aforementioned plots I, J, and K. John Palmer sold this eight-acre parcel to Baker Sniffen in 1855. Sniffen later divided it, selling the north four to Isaac Sarles in 1856 and retaining the south four for himself. This property was then combined with plots I, J, and K when Orson Sarles sold to Ann and James Outhouse, and it was included in the subsequent sales to Malone and then to Swope.

Teatown Lake was built by Gerard Swope Sr. in 1924. Although early deeds refer to this land as being farmed and even mention a "big meadow," it was apparently all red maple swamp by the time the lake was built. Henry Bell, who had worked at the Croft even in Vernay's time, and his brother, Mahlon, were in charge of clearing the trees.

As you can see, the initial grants and subsequent division into individual farm holdings reflected the character of 19th-century Westchester County growth. It was not until Gerard Swope Sr. reversed the process that the Teatown area began to more closely resemble what this part of the world looked like in its original state. With the 20th century, a new concern for the preservation of unspoiled nature came like a breath of fresh air to the United States. Environmental philanthropy was on its way.

John Palmer's barn, pictured c. 1920, stood near today's maple sugarhouse.

Local dairy farmers used this milk depository on Spring Valley Road for temporary cold storage before transport to New York City. (Photograph by Helen Arbor Young.)

Shown is the William Palmer House, at 400 Blinn Road. (Photograph by Chuck Davidson.)

Six

DIGGING UP THE PAST

Essay by Ken Soltesz

When hiking the trails of Teatown, you cannot help but wonder about the ancient stone walls and foundations that still stand today as solemn remnants of a distant past. Who built these structures? Who lived and worked on this land? How different were their lives from ours today?

Although some of these questions may remain forever unanswered, a lot can be learned from such recorded documents as property deeds, mortgages, tax maps, and census reports. Anyone who has ever visited the Land Documents Division of the Westchester County Clerk's Office in White Plains knows it to be something of a madhouse. Hundreds of real estate runners pick up a battery of phones for one another, yelling the caller's name across the enormous room filled with shelf upon shelf of huge volumes dating back to the American Revolution, ready for copying on a bank of machinery. Here is where all the documents relating to land transfers in the Teatown area are located. It is an atmosphere in startling contrast to the peaceful surroundings of the reservation itself.

Research conducted by the author in 1986 revealed many secrets of Teatown's past. In Colonial times, most of present-day Teatown—all of the land around Teatown Lake and the Hidden Valley area—was an orchard and dairy farm for a Van Cortlandt tenant. In 1750, the Van Cortlandts established a farmstead in the area, which still exists today at 400 Blinn Road, about a half mile northwest of Spring Valley Road. Blinn Road then was simply a lane through the woods ending at the farmhouse.

When Van Cortlandt Manor was divided up and sold off in the 1780s, much of the Teatown area was bought by William Palmer from the Van Cortlandt heirs. The first U.S. census (1790) shows Palmer and his wife, Mary, and a daughter living on the farmstead. Three more children, all boys, were born to the Palmers. They eventually inherited roughly equal portions of their father's land. The family continued as prominent landholders for more than 100 years.

The Lakeside Trail, leading from the Tudor administration buildings to the Teatown Lake dam, crosses land referred to in an early deed as the Big Meadow. The meadow was flooded when Teatown Lake was constructed in 1924. On the section of the trail southwest of the dam, you come upon a pair of old farmhouse foundations. This was the farmstead of Richard Palmer, one of William Palmer's sons. He worked his farm for only a decade, after which it passed to a succession of owners. These houses were standing as recently as 1915. Daylilies, popular garden flowers during the 1800s, still bloom at this site. Continuing on the Lakeside Trail down to the south shore of Teatown Lake, you can see the remains of an old house foundation between the lake and Spring Valley Road (No. 1685). This was part of the Kahrs farm, which included land now submerged beneath the west end of Teatown Lake, as well as property south of Spring Valley Road. The house stood at this site until the 1930s.

The red house at the junction of Spring Valley Road and Blinn Road (No. 1560) was part of the five-acre dairy farm from 1868 to the 1930s. The foundation of the dairy farm is still visible beside the driveway. This driveway was retained by the Palmers for dry access to their fields, thus avoiding the marsh along Blinn Road. The large spreading sugar maple at the north end of the driveway long provided a shady refuge for the workers, who mowed the fields by hand, and the tree came to be known as the Mower's Maple. A partial increment boring taken in 1985 showed the tree to be about 150 years old.

When Gerard Swope Sr. purchased and merged all these properties in the 1920s, the era of farming came to an end. However, those of us who enjoy the scenic trails of Teatown will always admire the old walls and foundations and be reminded of the early families that lived and worked on this beautiful land.

Haying at the Croft is Albert Whitfield (on the hay wagon), superintendent of the Croft from 1927 to 1957. Henrietta Swope is in the background.

Arthur and Marion Vernay pose during construction of the Croft in 1913.

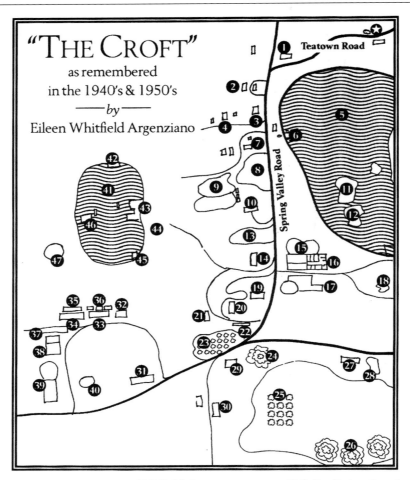

"THE CROFT"

as remembered in the 1940's & 1950's
— by —
Eileen Whitfield Argenziano

Teatown Road

Spring Valley Road

★ Where a metorite made a big hole

1. Kimball's home
2. Brown's home (painted angles on ceiling)
3. McCullen's home (she smoked a pipe and rolled her own cigerettes)
4. Nye's home (weekend place and summer retreat, well and a latern)
5. Teatown Lake
6. Dock for boats
7. Whitfield's home
8. Cornfield and gardens
9. Fruit Orchards (Pears, apples, plums, peaches, grapes and beehives)
10. David Swope Sr.'s home
11. Treasure Island
12. Mystery Island
13. Strawberry patch and root cellar
14. Waterlily pond

15. Paddock for horses
16. Carriage house and stable
17. Studio
18. Estate jump
19. David Swope Sr.'s Home
20. Garage, laundry room and two apartments for help
21. Green house
22. Tennis court
23. Vegetable garden
24. Large sweet cherry tree
25. Berry patch
26. Sour cherry trees
27. Gerard Swope Jr.'s home
28. Blueberry pone
29. Small house (Spedial, Howe, Purdy)
30. Morris's home (State trooper garage and stable for Mr. Jackson)

31. Ord. boarding house for employees
32. Ice house
33. Hay barn
34. Cow Barn and milk house
35. Pig stye
36. Bee hives
37. Garage and wood shed
38. Honey house and garage
39. Chicken house and run
40. Baby chicken coop
41. Vernay Lake
42. Dam
43. Swimming area, bathhouses and boat house
44. Tea house
45. Water pump
46. Employee swimming area and raft
47. Water tower

This map of the Croft shows where a meteorite hit (starred) as well as 47 other identified places (numbered).

Seven

RESERVATION PRESERVATION

"To conserve open space and to educate and involve the regional community in order to sustain the diversity of wildlife, plants, and habitats for future generations."—Teatown's mission.

Gerard Swope Sr., who lived in New York City, sought a country retreat for his growing family. He was responsible for assembling an estate that today forms the nucleus of Teatown Lake Reservation, located in the southwestern corner of the town of Yorktown in Westchester County, New York. The converted stable and carriage house across Spring Valley Road from his house now serve as Teatown's administrative center. In 1988, to celebrate Teatown's 25th anniversary, the buildings were expanded in Tudor style but completely modernized.

Swope, son of immigrant parents, was born in 1872. A graduate of Massachusetts Institute of Technology, he began his professional career in a low-level position—"a dirty, oily job"—with Western Electric in Chicago. After completing important service at the World War I War Industries Board in Washington, D.C., he was lured away from Western Electric to become president of International General Electric. From that post he became president of GE in 1922. Under his direction, the company began extensive manufacture of electric appliances for home use. It is said that the first electric blanket was presented to Swope by GE engineers who had learned of his predilection for sleeping on an open porch during the winter. Swope was also closely identified with the development of radio and its accessories. He was a director of the National Broadcasting Company (jointly owned by GE and Westinghouse) and was also a director of 14 other companies associated with the electric and power industries.

In 1939, after 18 years as president of GE, Swope reached the retirement age of 67 and relinquished the office. He thereupon entered public service as chairman of the New York City Housing Authority, a full-time job paying $1 a year. He left that post in 1942 to resume the presidency of GE when its current president went off to war. At war's end he was elected honorary president of GE. He was the recipient of countless honors and medals for his pioneering leadership in various fields of public service. He was a member of the Westchester County Park System Board of Commissioners.

While still at GE, Swope commuted to Manhattan, regularly enjoying a relaxed breakfast on the last leg of the *Twentieth Century Limited*'s dining-car service. Upon his retirement, the Croft became his year-round residence. In every kind of weather, Swope, an avid horseman, rode the far-flung trails on his property (now Teatown's walking paths) and reveled in the natural world around him. He helped establish the Dirt Trails Association, a dues-paying group of northern Westchester equestrian landowners, who maintained horse trails and rode through private property as far south as Tarrytown and east to Connecticut. The experience proved useful as a model of private land for public use.

As a young adult in Chicago, working in his off-hours as a volunteer at Hull House, the famous settlement house for immigrant education and culture, Swope met and married fellow social worker Mary Dayton Hill. Together, they taught classes and gave support to new arrivals in this country. After marriage and moving to New York City and the Croft, they raised five children: Isaac, Henrietta, John, and twins David and Gerard Jr. (affectionately known as Jerry).

It may be said of Gerard Swope Sr. that he had a keen sense of social responsibility. His relations with labor while he served at GE through a terrible Depression were exemplary. Because of the Swopes' love of the outdoors and their appreciation of natural beauty combined with their high sense of public obligation, they would have smiled when events following their deaths gave the people of Westchester a magnificent not-for-profit nature preserve.

This is how it happened.

Long before the world became immersed in concepts of ecological awareness, Gerard and Mary Swope were consciously engaged in environmental preservation, reversing a long history of property fragmentation in the Teatown area. Indeed, one might say that the Swope family proceeded to put back together what William Palmer had torn asunder in 1832. In 1924, Swope dammed the brook running through his low-lying meadows and swamps to create the shallow but beautiful 33-acre Teatown Lake. He also added adjoining properties to his original purchase as parcels became available. The tradition continues; in recent years, the Reservation has purchased key tracts of special ecological interest. They include a large parcel of woods behind Spring Valley Road, a substantial acreage overlooking and draining Hidden Valley, and the management, on behalf of the Open Space Institute, of another large tract on the northernmost slopes above Hidden Valley.

When Swope died in 1957, he bequeathed all the Croft properties in even shares to his four surviving children and widowed daughter-in-law, with no specific instructions as to how the land was to be used. Together the heirs decided to transfer the property to some type of public agency. The intention was simply that it be put to some sort of public use.

Initial contact was made with Westchester County, which declined to take over ownership of the land without a substantial endowment. Through Richard Pough, chairman of the Nature Conservancy, a meeting was arranged between Gerard Swope Jr., acting for the heirs, and the Brooklyn Botanic Garden (BBG). BBG had already wet its feet locally by accepting from the Van Brunt family stewardship of a 223-acre parcel of land two miles east of Teatown on Kitchawan Road. BBG erected on the site a biological laboratory, which became known as the Kitchawan Station.

With Kitchawan as a model, intricate negotiations commenced between Gerard Swope and the BBG Board of Directors. The land transfer was finalized on December 20, 1963. The future of Teatown Lake Reservation was placed in the hands of five directors. They were Gerard Swope Jr.; his twin brother, David, a prominent Westchester developer; and three members of the BBG Board of Governors. BBG agreed to underwrite the cost of maintaining the property in its current shape and to pay the salaries of personnel who might be hired. It also reserved the right to sell the land but granted Westchester County and Yorktown rights of first refusal. BBG, a long-established horticultural organization, concluded its acceptance meeting with the words of its chairman, H.J. Szold: "You are conferring future enjoyment on people you don't know, and people who are yet to come. It is a kind of deferred annuity of Nature."

Besides giving financial support, BBG was not intensely involved in Teatown's operation and general activities; that was best left to the neighborhood. Gerard Swope Jr. became the moving spirit behind Teatown. After retiring as international counsel for GE, he devoted himself to the reservation and helped to make it an educational center. He lived a few minutes' walk away on a parcel of land whose history is outlined in chapter four. Like his father before him, he dammed a stream across his property, creating Blueberry Pond. Early on, the Cortlandt Conservation Association evinced an interest in Teatown's development and helped BBG start the first nature classes for children. The first naturalist was Warren Balgooyen, who served the reservation for 20 years. Swope always liked to say that "Warren just came down the road from Kitchawan," where he had been a staff member. Balgooyen became a truly beloved Teatowner, leaving an unmistakable imprint on the reservation. Of equal importance were the neighbors, the volunteers, and the steering committee led by Katie Little, who performed countless educational guidance and maintenance chores, and mounted exhibits and marvelous country fairs. These "Teatown toilers" were an important part of the reservation and helped make it a flourishing community experience.

In 1971, when Teatown Lake Reservation was formally incorporated, the five-man board was replaced by a new 21-member board of directors, including four officers. The reservation's new legal status made it easier to develop individual and corporate contributions and to create a substantial endowment. However, the days of BBG's contributions were numbered due to a growing fiscal crisis in New York City. If the 1960s were the years of Teatown's initial growth and the 1970s its adolescence, the decades since have mirrored its mature acceptance as a long-lived community resource.

The time arrived when it became both wise and expedient for Teatown to come out from under the skirt of BBG as an independent entity. This belief was underlined in a series of amicable discussions between members of both boards, which concluded with an agreement granting Teatown independence, a situation that continues to this day.

Gerard Swope Jr. died in 1979, just as Teatown's representatives were crossing the t's and dotting the i's of the final separation agreement. Both boards continued to exchange ex-officio members. Teatown's formal Independence Day came on July 4, 1987.

Teatown Lake Reservation has become a community center, as well as a nature and environmental center. Its various volunteer activities bring people closer together in working for a common goal. In 1990, a substantial bequest by the late Marion Rosenwald Ascoli, a Teatown trustee, added Cliffdale Farm—160 acres of beautiful, rolling farmland and deep woods and trails—to Teatown's stockpile of natural enjoyment. With its track record of success, now measured in an enrollment of 1,800 members, a bright future for Teatown Lake Reservation seems assured.

This aerial view shows Teatown Lake in 1972. (Photograph by Tom Woods.)

The Swopes pause for a family portrait c. 1948. Pictured, from left to right, are the following: (front row) Topo, John, Dorry, David, David Jr., and Gerard Jr.; (back row) Lucy, Ike, Mary, Gerard Sr., and Henrietta.

After their father's death in 1957, Gerard Swope Jr. (1905–1979), shown here, and his twin brother, David, were instrumental in working out the complex transfer of most of the Croft properties to the Brooklyn Botanic Garden as an outreach station and nature preserve. Following his retirement as international counsel for GE, Jerry was, until his death, a major guardian angel for the reservation.

Working closely with all the Swope heirs, David Swope (1905–1980), shown here, helped facilitate the creation of Teatown Lake Reservation. Once the governing body was in place, David became and remained an active trustee of the reservation until his death.

The Swope family joins Croft families at the annual Christmas party in the carriage house in 1945.

Warren Balgooyen (left) and Gerard Swope Jr. team up at the sugarhouse.

A volunteer work crew, organized by Peter Oldenberg, constructs a wetland boardwalk over Bailey Brook through Griffen Swamp in 1981.

The waters of Bailey Brook rush downstream. (Photograph by Peter Oldenberg.)

A concert of baroque music is performed at the boathouse in 1973, with Lloyd Moss as host.

Folk singer Pete Seeger performs at the boathouse in 1989.

Mandy Thompson and former Teatown naturalist Mark Spreyer attend the Winter Weekend square dance *c.* 1980.

The annual Teatown Fishing Derby is the one day that fishing is permitted at the reservation.

Ice hockey teams compete on Teatown Lake during Winter Weekend in 1976.

Another feature of Winter Weekend is the sleigh ride, as shown in this 1976 photograph.

Eileen Argenziano, who chaired many of the early Teatown fairs, is pictured in 1968.

Teatown trustee and former board chairman Geoff Thompson (far right) makes apple cider at the Teatown Fall Festival.

Former naturalist Ken Soltesz presses cider at the 1984 Fall Festival.

The 1985 Teatown Fall Festival is in full swing.

One of the most popular family events of the Fall Festival is the Pumpkin Carve. (Poster by Chuck Davidson.)

The Pumpkin Carve is under way at the Teatown Fall Festival. (Photograph by Mary Ann Van Hengel.)

Linda Cooper, Yorktown supervisor, and her husband, Peter Cooper, attend Teatown's biannual Night in the Woods gala. Linda has been an active Teatown volunteer since she was a teenager and has served many years as a trustee.

Attendees peruse the display tables during the 2002 Night in the Woods gala. Held at the home of John and Janet DeVito, this biannual event, chaired by trustees DJ Chain and Dena Thomas, has become a major Teatown fundraiser.

Participating in Teatown's annual plant sale are former staff members Rod Christie (left) and Dave Fermoile (center) with current staff member Phyllis Bock in 2002.

During Teatown's annual plant sale, volunteers Libby Mossman (left) and Celia Carroll welcome shoppers to the herbs section.

In this 1976 photograph, Warren Balgooyen pours maple sap into Teatown's first evaporator.

Eight

SWEET TIDINGS

Essay by Phyllis Bock

Sap's rising—it's sugaring time! For hundreds of years, the coming of spring was heralded not by the first robin catching a worm on the front lawn but by the slow drip of maple sap filling a bucket with sweet liquid. Even before the *Mayflower* touched shore, native people of the eastern woodlands counted on the gift of the maples to sustain them through the last hardship days of winter.

A drive along Spring Valley Road or Blinn Road tells a story about Teatown's sugaring history. Testaments to an earlier era are the many sugar maples that line these roads. Sugar maples are often the largest trees standing, indications that the farmers who cleared these forests to raise cows or plant fields also knew that maples yielded a cash crop. It is not hard to imagine a horse-drawn sledge winding along snow-covered lanes, hauling the sap to a family sugaring operation. As a naturalist, I get to experience firsthand the joys and hard work of sugaring season, an experience I had relegated to favorite books and New England farms.

Modern-day sugaring at Teatown began with its first director, Warren Balgooyen. With a keen interest in homesteading and pioneer skills, Balgooyen quickly realized the potential sugaring offered for learning. From tapping a few maples, collecting sap by hand, and boiling it over an open fire, to the first small evaporator located in the old cider shed, Balgooyen tied together education and history. Certainly his sugarhouse, with its moss-covered roof and jauntily tilted chimney, is a reminder of how the history of the land can be a powerful tool in teaching about today's environment.

Built in 1976 from woods culled from the property, the sugarhouse delights the many visitors that enter its doors. The shakes were hand split from white and red cedar, sassafras, and oak—all trees known for their rot-resistant properties. Looking up at the rafters 25 years later, you can still see the adze marks on the beams. The littlest of children sometimes have to be coaxed inside; the dark interior and glowing fire stir up images of fairy tales told at bedtime.

Many people contributed to Teatown's sugaring operation. Todd Baldwin, Teatown's forester in the 1980s, caught "sugaring fever" and expanded the sugarbush, tapping trees at Cliffdale and in Hidden Valley. Good forestry techniques meant thinning the woodlands to allow the sugar maples to expand their crowns and grow. Nights in the sugarhouse waiting for the sap to boil down, with volunteers such as Willie Shampnoi, were a time for swapping yarns and keeping curious critters away. They must have laughed when a hungry raccoon stopping in for a sweet treat got chased into the rafters by Baldwin's dog.

My introduction to Teatown came from my personal sugarmeister, Dave Fermoile, who kept the fire going in the sugarhouse through 10 seasons. Senior naturalist at Teatown in the 1990s, his brand of sugaring was to invite everyone in to share stories, music, and laughter. Youngsters hesitant to try something new were always encouraged and came away excited about their experience.

There are certain days at Teatown when everything feels just right. Those days are often during late winter, when red-winged blackbirds come back and the snow covering the ground begins to melt. You step outside and hear not only the *conkaree* of the blackbirds but the slightly metallic sound of sap pinging into buckets. Then the connection is made: history and nature come together during a very short but sweet season. Days are filled with the sharp scent of wood fires, the sweet aroma of maple syrup, the soft sight of steam garlanding the rafters of the sugarhouse, and the happy voices of children echoing with the joy of new discoveries.

A little bit more sky shows through the cedar shakes of Balgooyen's sugarhouse now, but on a frosty starlit night in March, with the fire glowing, the steam rising, and the sap boiling, there is no place I would rather be.

It is time to inspect the maple sugar buckets. (Photograph by Maria Karsanidi.)

Warren Balgooyen's sugarhouse stands alone in the woods. (Photograph by Lois Barker.)

A pancake breakfast, with plenty of maple syrup, is held in the carriage house.

The field by Spring Valley Road is the place to study butterflies and insects. These students are attending Teatown's summer camp.

54

Nine

CHILD'S PLAY

Essay by Rod Christie

We all have a person who makes a lasting impression on our lives—a father, a mother, a mentor, a teacher. Mine was my mother. She was the one who turned over rocks and showed me what was underneath. She shared with me her knowledge of animals and how to handle them and care for their needs. She let me wallow in the mud and bring tadpoles home to raise. She was my companion in exploration.

Over the years, we caught turtles together, cared for any orphaned or injured creature, and explored every inch of most habitats around our house. She taught me a great deal, but the most important thing I learned by example—a reverence for life. She taught me the value of the tiniest and most reviled creature. She engrained in me a system of values that was predicated on putting aside my needs and protecting all things wild, regardless of their stature or the level of their interference.

So how does my childhood relate to the history of Teatown? Throughout Teatown's existence, the staff has striven to do for children just what my mother did for me. When I appeared on the Teatown scene, I was asked to build on an already quality educational program and expand it to serve an increasing demand from the community. My first duty was to turn the old horse stall, complete with a well-chewed stall door, into my office. This meant extracting the mounted dead animals, bones, shells, and other sundries stored there and convincing the mice that I was there to stay. I still have a vivid memory of the abandoned stall next to me, which was splattered with whitewash and feathers from the previous resident. It was the beginning of a chronology of experiences that would do justice to the term "unique working conditions."

In the next few years, we expanded programming to include the establishment of Teatown's popular summer camp, an expansion to the school program, and a more diverse slate of weekend public offerings. An integral part of Teatown's success during those early years was the efforts of many talented volunteers and dedicated staff such as Mimi Shane and Dottie Metzler. With time, our program was enhanced with the added strengths of new naturalists, including Dave Fermoile, Phyllis Bock, Paul Miethner, Andrea Sauro, Terry Kardos, Emily Leveen, Wendy Nufer, and others—names synonymous with enthusiasm and the ability to relate to children. These gifted naturalists took children beyond their inherent love of exploration to a real understanding of the many delicate relationships that exist in the natural world. From Knee-Hi Nature to summer camp, the Teatown staff worked together over those years to forge a program that continues today to connect children with the essence of the outdoor world. An example helps to illustrate our approach.

Children inherently love to catch things, and Teatown's staff often used this enthusiasm to get them digging into the ponds, looking under logs, or netting insects in the field. Getting children involved was the easy part; stopping them from pillaging the landscape was the challenge. One way we could limit the damage was to set prerequisites. "Before you go and catch frogs, you need to build them a habitat, complete with everything they need to survive. What do they need and how much? Are they predators or prey? Are they herbivores or carnivores?" All these questions needed to be answered and acted upon before the catching began. The children had to keep in mind how many frogs their habitat could hold. "We can catch a lot, but we'd better keep only one. Don't put that big frog with that small one, or you know what'll happen!" What at first glance looked like a simple trip to the pond became an intricate lesson in ecology.

In my later years at Teatown, the acquisition of Cliffdale Farm brought new opportunities. After much discussion, it was decided to move the Native American program there and construct a small encampment. John Shull, a local archaeologist and friend of mine, used tulip trees felled on the property and other natural materials to construct two wigwams and a longhouse. Later, we added a garden and other features. Native American culture was an important part of our programming because it taught the children about how early Americans respected the land and rarely abused it, in contrast to the more dramatic changes associated with the arrival of the first settlers. Cliffdale was also a perfect location for investigating life on a small farm. Some of the more traditional endeavors included making ice cream, spinning wool, collecting eggs, and making apple cider. Some of the more unusual but just as tactile activities were prodding the ducks for oil from their oil glands, and testing our skills at cow-chip tossing (ah, the simple pleasures of life on the farm).

The most difficult thing about educating children is gauging your impact. Are you making a difference in the world and helping to build more environmentally conscious adults? To this I say yes. I still have people I taught as children come back to tell me where they are and what an influence I had on their lives. What is even more surprising is that often it is not those children I remember the most; often it is the hyperactive child, going through a difficult time in life, who received in a nonconventional atmosphere like Teatown's just the stability needed to make learning more palatable. A friend and great educator once told me that he believed many children "learn from chaos," and I think this is true. Children who have lots of stimulating things going on around them pick and choose what they want to remember, and we as teachers rarely know what tidbit will sink in. As teachers at Teatown, we often stressed principles and "facts," but our greatest and most enduring strength was the cornucopia of natural experiences that we made available.

Even the complex study of grasses is made interesting.

Surrounded by a group of fascinated children, Francie Elwyn (right) teaches local geology c. 1969.

Kaye Anderson (third from the right), a former Teatown naturalist, is pictured c. 1975.

october 17, 1975

Dear Teatown Friends

I liked the nature trail and

the movie and all the animel

and one goat Trid to Eat My

Post card.

From

Brendan

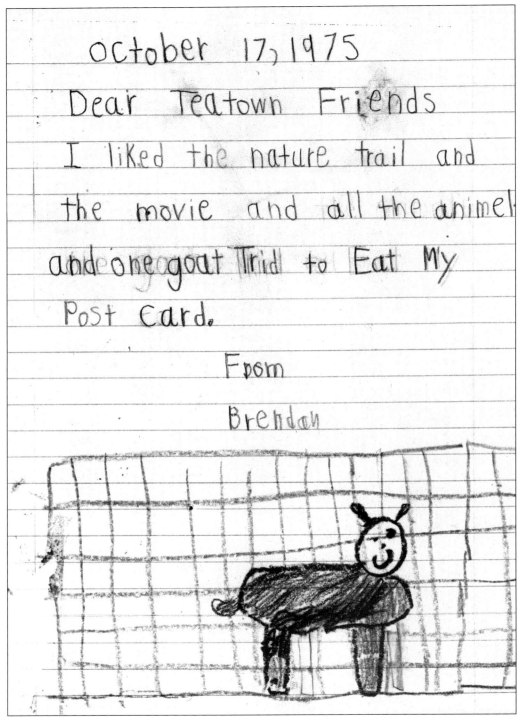

This charming letter from Brendan includes a drawing of the Teatown goat. Addressed to "Teatown Friends," it was written on October 17, 1975.

Patches the goat, seen here in 1975, was popular even though he ate everything—lunches, exhibits, bills, and letters.

Naturalist Henry Burke leads a class on a bird walk in 2000.

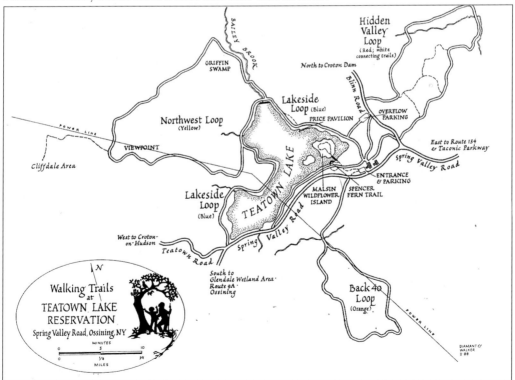

This 1980 map shows the walking trails at Teatown. (Map by Barbara Walker and Lincoln Diamant.)

Shari Vice, Teatown's volunteer coordinator, is shown in 1999 among the sunflowers in the Three Sisters Garden at Cliffdale Farm.

Gene Lagonia (center), Teatown's facilities manager, works with the maintenance crew to restore the Bergmann Boardwalk in 2000.

There is always time for quiet contemplation and writing a special poem. A rock makes a good seat.

Children are participating in a pond study class at the boathouse. (Photograph by Ellan Young.)

A child peers inside a butterfly net.

Regardless of weather, yellow school buses deliver excited children to Teatown nearly every weekday.

Students gather around a hole cut in the ice to study the pond in winter. One of the winter experiments tests the turbidity of the lake.

Volunteer Micky Spano (left) works with a group of students.

Former naturalist Colleen McGrath (right) shows students that a rock can make a good classroom.

Some fourth- and fifth-graders start off on a bike trip with Ed Kanze (left) in 1983 as part of the junior naturalists program.

Ossining teacher John Boyle (left) and Andrew Keyes examine a snapping turtle in a research project to map the turtle population in Teatown Lake. The photograph was taken in 1985.

The year-round Mommy and Me program was started by volunteer Patti Malone in 1988.

In this 2002 photograph, naturalist Amy Keith helps out at a birthday party, a popular event at Teatown.

With a group of children, former naturalist David Fermoile looks through a net in 1998.

This shows a hands-on (eek!) experience.

Naturalist Emily Leveen (center) works with children from the Ossining Recreation Department after-school program in 2000. This program was supported through a grant from the National Recreation Foundation to serve underprivileged children.

High school student Alison Malone samples a stream in 2002. Data collected through this water quality program at Teatown is used by local planning departments and the county.

Former education director Dottie Metzler prepares one of Teatown's videos in 1983.

Ruth Rubenstein (front left), director of education, leads an adult field trip through the Shawangunk mountain range, southeast of the Catskills, in 2001.

Volunteer Alison Beal (center, back to camera) trains a group of future guides in 1987. The guide program was started in 1972.

Many senior citizen groups take advantage of Teatown's extensive trails.

Marion Rosenwald Ascoli, a principal benefactor of Teatown Lake Reservation, goes for a walk at Cliffdale Farm *c.* 1983.

The buildings at Cliffdale Farm reflect past and present uses of the land.

This open gate leads to the rolling fields of Cliffdale Farm.

Teatown trustees, from left to right, Michael Weiner, Alice Bamberger, Marguerite Pitts, Lincoln Diamant, and Bill Arnold take part in the dedication of Cliffdale Farm in 1991.

At Cliffdale Farm, farmer Tim Gilbert and farm educator Susanna Gilbert have been teaching children of all ages about conserving rare breeds of farm animals. They are shown in 1998.

Bo and Honey were part of the Teatown menagerie.

Shown in 2002 at Cliffdale Farm are Holly Athas and Sally the cow.

At Cliffdale Farm, chickens are a favorite with summer campers. (Photograph by Lois Barker.)

Wildlife photographer Leonard Lee Rue III captivates his audience at a Teatown program on wolves in 1977.

Famed anthropologist and Teatown lecturer Richard Leakey (left) answers questions on the ascent of man to Lincoln Diamant in 1978. (Photograph by Nadine B. Stearns.)

World-famous microbiologist and Pulitzer Prize winner Dr. René Dubos lectures at Teatown. He popularized the phrase "Think globally, act locally."

A northeastern gypsy moth-control conference takes place at Teatown in 1980. Many environmental conferences have been held here throughout the decades, covering such topics as Lyme disease, deer control, lake eutrophication, clean water, and open space protection.

A bluebird alights with a meal in its beak. Bluebird houses are placed in the meadow off Blinn Road and throughout the fields at Cliffdale Farm.

Ten

WINGING IT

Essay by Edward Kanze

An entire 18 years have come and gone since I lived and worked beside the shore of Teatown Lake. During that interval, I have watched birds from Maine to Mississippi, from the roadrunner-crowded scrub of Big Bend National Park in Texas to the kiwi and emu-haunted landscapes of New Zealand and Australia. Still, I can think of no more agreeable and profitable place to watch birds than Teatown, no place where birds and bird watchers are more likely to felicitously converge.

Spring offers the height of glamour. This is the time of year when you can walk from the nature museum down the hill to the boathouse and beyond to the dam and Bailey Brook and count on seeing, depending on the date and the progress of that particular season, enough species to overwhelm a beginner. I remember leading bird walks down this path on sunny May mornings. We would take in the bright colors of yellow-rumped warblers and American redstarts, note a catbird mewing in the bushes near the bird blind, hear a blue-winged warbler buzzing in the parking field (sometimes accompanied by a bluebird), and take in the thin, high piping of a love-struck brown creeper, rising from the oak-hickory woods east of the lakeshore.

If the year brought a spike in the numbers of hairy caterpillars, there might be cuckoos, too. My first year at Teatown, 1981, saw the woods alive with yellow-billed and black-billed cuckoos, uttering weird, guttural songs when they were not wolfing down gypsy moth larvae and tent caterpillars.

Down Bailey Brook, a little stroll below the dam, on the trail toward Griffin Swamp, the spirit of spring is summed up by the Louisiana waterthrush. I first learned to recognize this bird's song at Teatown. Now, I cannot imagine life without it. The drab bird, small and brown of back with a streaked belly, arrives in late April. "*Here, here, here,*" it begins, with three sharp whistles. Then, it segues into exuberant self-promotion: "Listen, 'cause I'm wonderfully musical!" It sings for prospective mates, not for the rest of us, but many a happy morning, a group of regulars and I stood on the sidelines, relishing the performance.

These birds and dozens more can be seen and heard in spring, a season when a rare find may also turn up, such as the golden-winged warbler that greeted us one morning on the Back 40 Trail. Yet, there is good news if you read these words after spring has come and gone. The pleasures of roaming the woods, meadows, and wetlands of Teatown, binoculars around one's neck, extend throughout the year.

Once, in winter, the temperature stood at zero when a morning bird walk was scheduled. Two young men showed up. They were eager to go, and I was caught in my personal version of the post office motto. Neither rain, nor sleet, nor numbing cold, I used to say, would keep me from my appointed rounds.

We went. We walked all the way to the old archery range near Blinn Road without seeing or hearing a single bird. Then, I looked up and gasped. A rough-legged hawk, the first and last I ever saw at Teatown, floated against a sky of the deepest blue. We all had grand looks and, in those quiet minutes, the outing was rendered a success.

The more I ponder, the more delicious moments flood back. I remember a night hike to Hidden Valley, when on the way back out to civilization we heard a barred owl blare, "*Who cooks for you? Who cooks for you-all?*" from branches directly overhead. There were times when broad-winged hawks, which nest at Teatown, circled low over us in the walnut meadow, uttering plaintive whistles, and joyous days in late winter when the silent lake exploded with the clamor of Canada geese and red-winged blackbirds.

Solitary adventures have their pleasures, but they can only rival, never exceed, the delights of exploring territory in congenial company. Teatown is a place where, if you set off alone to hunt for the yellow-bellied sapsucker, you are sure to meet a neighbor or make a new acquaintance whether or not you find your quarry. I loved those serendipities: exchanging warm hellos with Milton Berger, out taking his daily constitutional around the lake; meeting Bob Keyes or John Askildsen in the parking lot, and swapping news of warblers and vireos; and hauling myself out of bed at some cruel hour to meet Teatowners, such as the Arnolds and the Garrisons, the Diamants and Nelly Ballofet, Linda Cooper, and Patti Malone, who took the sting out of the alarm clock and made every organized bird walk at Teatown an experience to be savored.

Go into the woods. Look and listen for the birds. Make new friends and meet your neighbors. I envy you the pleasure.

Binoculars up! Ed Kanze (third from the left) leads a group of bird watchers during migration season in 1984. Kanze is a former Teatown naturalist. (Photograph by Sophie Keyes.)

Teatown Lake has a family of swans. (Photograph by Bernie Kessler.)

This immature green heron nests on Wildflower Island. (Photograph by Ed Kanze.)

Frosty the screech owl is part of Teatown's raptor education program. (Photograph by Ellan Young.)

This is Athena, a barred owl. The raptor education program began in 1991 with the arrival of Teatown's executive director, Gail Abrams. The program uses non-releasable birds of prey to educate the public about the necessity of conserving and protecting the natural habitats of these important predators. An outside exhibit area houses falcons, hawks, owls, and vultures in large wooden cages. Volunteers are trained to care for, feed, and handle each bird for education programs, as well as to monitor the bird's general health.

This broad-winged hawk, named Shadow, is part of the raptor education program.

The heart and the soul of Wildflower Island, Marjorie Swope (above) and Jane Darby (below), worked every day on this jewel of Teatown. These photographs were taken in 1990.

Eleven

A Walk with Wildflowers

Essay by Warren Balgooyen

A rich diversity of wildflowers adorns the walking trails at Teatown in early spring. Some highlight the trails en masse in a grand display. Other species are more solitary and peek out unexpectedly from behind a rock or log. These wildings are strung out along the trails like jewels in a necklace. For those who seek them out, there are uncommon species confined to special habitats that may be captured on film or simply enjoyed.

The trail along Bailey Brook cuts through the carpet of spring beauty—a small five-petaled white flower with pink pinstripes. Here, also, are scattered specimens of dwarf ginseng and wood anemone. Farther along the brook, where a little tributary stream crosses the path, you can find marsh marigold deep in the watery recesses of Griffin Swamp. Their bright yellow blooms accent the stream in places and brighten scattered pools of standing water elsewhere in the swamp. To the east, across Blinn Road, lies a different theater. Here, in the deeper shade and solitude of Hidden Valley, you encounter an extraordinary mass of wild leek covering nearly a half acre of the valley bottomland near the base of the south slope. From the trail that follows the base of the north side of the valley, you can see purple trillium and rue anemone.

There are rewarding paths to follow in many parts of the reservation, Glendale Wetland and Cliffdale Farm in particular, but the mother lode of wildflower diversity at Teatown, the diamond in the necklace, is surely Wildflower Island.

I will always remember that special June day in 1970 when I landed a canoe on the island's north shore and discovered a treasure chest of floral jewels. I took but a few steps and stumbled upon dozens of pink lady's-slippers in bloom. A short distance farther on, near the small island's height of land, were several wild columbine on display, along with a scattering of polypody ferns. At the opposite end of the island was a thicket of white swamp azalea. Nearby was a rich green carpet of ground pine *Lycopodium*. If the trails of greater Teatown wear an ephemeral necklace, this island is like a visit to Tiffany's. Here was a treasure that had to be shared, yet also needed to be preserved.

The solution was to build a bridge to the island—but a bridge with a gate. Visitors would be welcome but only with a guide. The rudimentary bridge I built was made of recycled lumber. My "engineering" had involved a hand winch, cable, and pulley mounted on a tall frame of sassafras logs. It was a crude affair that included a 10-foot section in the center that cranked up a drawbridge. One Sunday, a ladies' garden party stood waiting for the draw to be lowered. Suddenly the bridge section on which the women were standing in wait (and in weight, due to the numbers) gave way. There was a whoop and a splash, followed by what seemed an eternity of silence. Everyone was standing knee-deep in water—the women in their Sunday finery. When the stunned silence broke, it broke in laughter.

Soon afterward, a new bridge was built, of much improved design and materials. The vision and expertise of Louise Malsin offered strong inspiration. Her husband, Arthur, generously volunteered to oversee and fund the new bridge and interpretive gatehouse. Both structures were dedicated in memory of Louise Malsin. Before long, the island was offering an even richer diversity of native flowers.

Marjorie Swope took on supervision of the island in a big way. She became its de facto steward. After the initial plantings were established, Jane Darby also became involved and served for many years as island keeper. With their loving care, the island more than blossomed; it became a mecca for those who recognized and appreciated its unusual beauty.

In 1983, my final year at Teatown, I spent many halcyon days working on the island. Marjorie Swope continued her labors as long as she was able; Jane Darby followed her example.

It was a rare privilege to be in the company of so many fine people working toward a common goal. It remains a pleasure to recall those days. Like William Wordsworth in "The Daffodils," I shall always see Wildflower Island's treasures "Beside the lake, beneath the trees / Fluttering and dancing in the breeze . . . / What wealth the show to me had brought."

The new bridge carries visitors to the unique attraction of Teatown's Wildflower Island. (Photograph by Bernie Kessler.)

These iron gates opening onto the bridge to Wildflower Island were designed by volunteer Midge Arnold.

Before the new gatehouse was erected, this rustic drawbridge, built by Warren Balgooyen in 1974, welcomed visitors to Wildflower Island.

This gatehouse exhibit shows the ferns of Wildflower Island.

In this 1983 photograph, volunteers pull purple loosestrife from Wildflower Island in an effort to keep this invasive weed from filling in the lake.

Large-flowered trillium is found on Wildflower Island. (Photograph by Midge Arnold.)

Spring beauty is plentiful along Bailey Brook and Wildflower Island. (Photograph by Midge Arnold.)

Snow covers Teatown Lake. (Photograph by Peter Oldenberg.)

Twelve

LOOKING FORWARD

Essay by Geoffrey Thompson

Land conservation has been an integral part of Teatown Lake Reservation's history. The Swope family knew that the public would appreciate and enjoy this unique landscape. They had the foresight and willingness to give away a valuable asset that today might otherwise be another set of housing subdivisions.

Teatown's role as a conservator of open space has continued to build. In the 1990s, Cliffdale Farm, the property of the late Marion Ascoli, was added. As we entered the new millennium, the reservation found itself confronting intensive development pressure on adjacent lands. The Teatown Board of Trustees concluded that it was crucial for the reservation to commence an organized effort to conserve and protect tracts of open space in the Teatown area. These properties were then ranked in importance based on their impact on Teatown's existing lands and their vulnerability to development. From this effort emerged a plan.

Teatown has been careful to pursue various methods of protection, including conservation easements. Virtually all of the landowners Teatown representatives have spoken with expressed great interest in seeing their lands preserved and protected as open space rather than developed. This feeling of community spirit and genuine caring for the future of property makes Teatown's protection efforts possible.

Teatown has also established strong relationships with the state and county governments, with New York City watershed officials, and with other possible funding sources. The city's efforts to protect the Croton Reservoir have been important to Teatown's ability to move forward with its conservation program. The reservation has partnered with various agencies to protect the land. In one specific case, the city agreed to purchase a conservation easement on a 26-acre tract that Teatown purchased from private owners in the Hidden Valley area. This partnership allowed Teatown to recoup 90 percent of its initial outlay. The conservation effort for this single parcel took more than 10 years, an indication of the challenges land-protection efforts face.

Teatown has a long-held dream of creating a trail system linking city, county, and state properties with Teatown's trail network. Within the next two years, Teatown hopes to help create this trail system, which will allow hikers to traverse open space from the North County Trailway on the east to the Old Croton Aqueduct Trailway and the Hudson River Greenway system on the west. Trails could extend from Yonkers all the way to Teatown.

Those who first envisioned Teatown Lake Reservation would be proud to see it celebrating its 40th birthday. The Swope family, Marion Ascoli, and all the others who played a crucial role in the making of the reservation would be glad to know that their acts of generosity have provided the foundation upon which so much more has followed.

TEATOWN LAKE RESERVATION

1600 Spring Valley Road
Ossining, NY 10562
(914) 762-2912

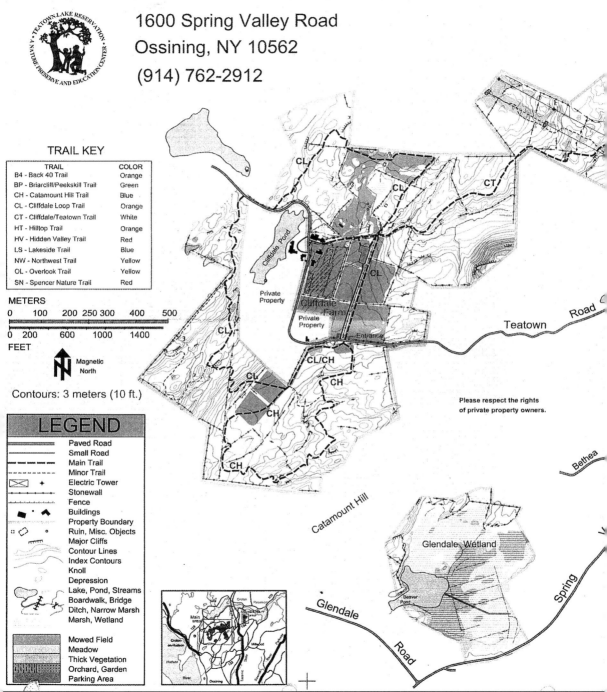

TRAIL KEY

TRAIL	COLOR
B4 - Back 40 Trail	Orange
BP - Briarcliff/Peekskill Trail	Green
CH - Catamount Hill Trail	Blue
CL - Cliffdale Loop Trail	Orange
CT - Cliffdale/Teatown Trail	White
HT - Hilltop Trail	Orange
HV - Hidden Valley Trail	Red
LS - Lakeside Trail	Blue
NW - Northwest Trail	Yellow
OL - Overlook Trail	Yellow
SN - Spencer Nature Trail	Red

METERS

0   100   200 250 300   400   500

0   200   600   1000   1400

FEET

Magnetic North

Contours: 3 meters (10 ft.)

LEGEND

	Paved Road
	Small Road
	Main Trail
	Minor Trail
	Electric Tower
	Stonewall
	Fence
	Buildings
	Property Boundary
	Ruin, Misc. Objects
	Major Cliffs
	Contour Lines
	Index Contours
	Knoll
	Depression
	Lake, Pond, Streams
	Boardwalk, Bridge
	Ditch, Narrow Marsh
	Marsh, Wetland
	Mowed Field
	Meadow
	Thick Vegetation
	Orchard, Garden
	Parking Area

Please respect the rights of private property owners.

This map of the reservation shows the roads, trails, buildings, bodies of water, and boundaries.

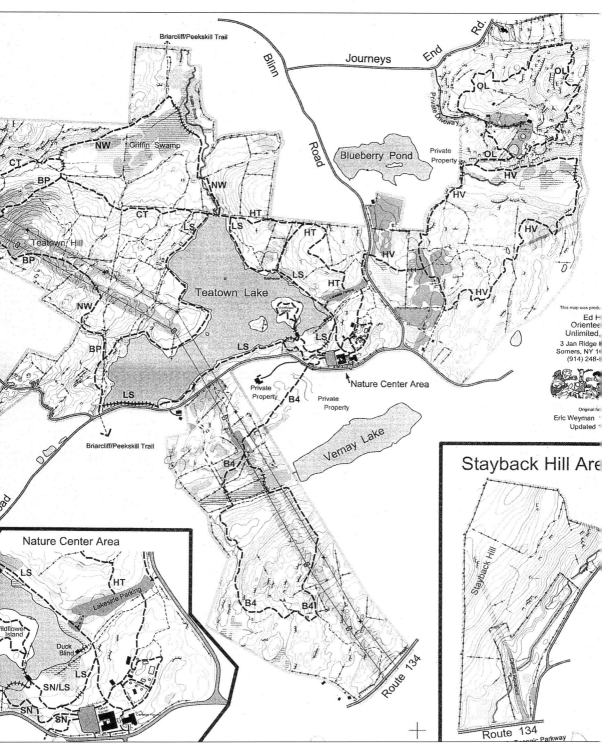

(Map courtesy Orienteering Unlimited Inc., Ed Hicks.)

CONTRIBUTORS

Gail Abrams, executive director since 1991, started Teatown's raptor education program. She has guided an expanding Teatown Lake Reservation into the 21st century.

Eileen Whitfield Argenziano, who grew up in the area, organized the first Teatown fair in 1965, with proceeds going toward a lake weed cutter. She chaired this annual event for 10 years, raising more than $100,000.

Midge Arnold has been a volunteer since the nature center began, primarily making exhibits for the carriage house, tending Wildflower Island, and creating a topographic model of the reservation.

Warren Balgooyen served Teatown as director and naturalist for 20 years. He is currently a director of the Norcross Foundation.

Phyllis Bock, a naturalist at Teatown since 1991, coordinates Teatown's school program, leads the volunteer nature guides, and codirects the summer camp program.

Jean Cameron-Smith, a real estate agent, writer, business owner, and Teatown neighbor, chairs the Teatown History Committee and is a trustee.

Rod Christie, now with Mianus Gorge Conservancy, served 11 years as Teatown's director of education.

Charles (Chuck) Davidson, a designer and creative director, has been involved with Teatown for more than two decades. He lives on the farmstead established by the Van Cortlandts in 1750.

Lincoln Diamant is the author of five history books on the American Revolution in the Hudson Valley and was the first president of Teatown.

Ellen Elchlepp has been an art director for more than 20 years and is a Teatown trustee.

Susan Jeffers, an award-winning artist of children's books, lives in the Teatown area.

Edward Kanze, a former senior naturalist at Teatown, is a travel writer and biographer of John Burroughs.

Sophie Keyes, a former trustee, was chair of Teatown's volunteer education guides.

Sandy Koppen, a member of Teatown for 30 years, chaired the 25th-anniversary celebration.

West Moss is a freelance writer and film editor who grew up on Teatown Road. She spent much of her childhood exploring the reservation.

Ruth Rubenstein, director of education at Teatown, is a published author and professional archaeologist, with a master's degree in anthropology.

Kenneth Soltesz, a former senior naturalist at Teatown, is curator of Westchester County's Cranberry Lake Preserve.

Geoffrey Thompson grew up in Croton and has lived in the Teatown neighborhood for 30 years. He has served Teatown as both board president and chairman. As chair of the Teatown Land Committee, he has overseen Teatown Lake Reservation's land-protection initiative. He owns a 500-tree apple orchard adjacent to the reservation.

Ellan Young, a photographer, taught for many years at the State University of New York at Purchase and worked for the *New York Times*.

Warren Balgooyen carries maple sap to Teatown's sugarhouse.

This building (former stables and carriage house for the Croft) houses the nature center. (Photograph by Ellan Young.)

The carriage house (former studio and groom's quarters for the Croft) is one of the most picturesque buildings at Teatown. (Photograph by Ellan Young.)

Along the trail, a footbridge crosses the water where lily pads thrive. (Photograph by Bernie Kessler.)

Deer pause for a drink at Teatown Lake. (Photograph by Dick Budnick.)

Of the 250 different plant species growing on Wildflower Island, the pink lady's-slippers are the most popular. These wild orchids are an endangered species. (Photograph by Midge Arnold.)

This enchanting wildflower is a yellow lady's-slipper. (Photograph by Midge Arnold.)

A horse at Cliffdale Farm nibbles at grass. (Photograph by Maria Karsanidi.)

Sally the cow looks up to see who has interrupted her grazing. (Photograph by Ellan Young.)

Mist rises from the warm water of Teatown Lake. (Photograph by Joanne Sheffler.)

A pair of Canada geese have the lake to themselves. (Photograph by Peter Oldenberg.)

A well-worn footpath follows the curve of the lakeshore. (Photograph by Helen Arbor Young.)

A full assortment of crisp leaves carpets the pathway into the woods, which are aflame with autumn color. (Photograph by Ellan Young.)

Shadows fall across the snow on a clear wintry day. (Photograph by Maria Karsanidi.)

After a gentle snowfall, each branch holds its allotment of white. (Photograph by Ed Malsberg.)

Totally absorbed in their work, three students explore near the boathouse.

The fronds of the fern are about to open. (Photograph by Bernie Kessler.)

At this hour of the day, the lakeside is deserted except for one Canada goose. (Photograph by Dick Budnick.)

Marsh marigolds bloom at the water's edge on Wildflower Island. (Photograph by Midge Arnold.)

The blossoms of a Canada lily on Wildflower Island hang gracefully from their tall stems. (Photograph by Midge Arnold.)

A fringed polygola opens in full bloom on Wildflower Island. (Photograph by Midge Arnold.)

A swamp white azalea produces a dazzling blossom on Wildflower Island. (Photograph by Midge Arnold.)

A Canada goose opens its wings, and the stillness of the lake remains unbroken. (Photograph by Ellan Young.)

Taking advantage of a floating log, 11 turtles catch the sunlight on their shells. (Photograph by Dick Budnick.)